A sequel to his Lambda Award-winning *Beautiful Signor* and a finalist for the National Poetry Series, *Is There Room for Another Horse on Your Horse Ranch?* is Cyrus Cassells's ninth, most high-spirited book. These unabashed, man-of-the-world poems cast over a lifetime of romantic and erotic experience with ready-to-roll lyricism, humor, and brio. After the moral urgency and outcry of his last book, *The World That the Shooter Left Us,* this globe-trotting collection of valentines, set in several different countries, arrives as a delightful surprise. A joyous cosmopolitan getaway, *Is There Room for Another Horse on Your Horse Ranch?* seems destined to be hailed as an engaging same-sex classic.

"The passionate, sun-drenched poems of Cyrus Cassells's *Is There Room for Another Horse on your Horse Ranch?* invite us into well rendered worlds of love, lust, and beauty. Though he writes in American English, Cassells is a European poet; though he writes in our time, Cassells is a nineteenth-century Romantic poet. Who else could write work so unapologetic in its appetites, so sexy and urbane at the same time? Here we see him at his best—brazen, erotic, confident, and full of verve. In this brilliant collection, Cassells is the 'artful, persistent dreamer,' and reading his poems, we become one, too."

RICHIE HOFMANN
author of *A Hundred Lovers*

"Cyrus Cassells's newest collection is a sensory and emotional ecstasy. These poems form a melodic, earthy, and vibrant orchestra, each one keenly tuned to a particular resonance of rapture or grief. Cassells enlists the heart, the body, various landscapes and geographies—from olive groves to oceans—as accompaniments, no, accomplices, to journeys through 'the blood-red joy / of breathing.' Here is the music of defiant, delightful aliveness inviting us again and again into the being of our humanity, that reaches out to us— 'you be the dancer.'"

LAUREN K. ALLEYNE
author of *Difficult Fruit* and *Honeyfish*
and Executive Director, Furious Flower Poetry Center

"Cyrus Cassells's latest book best articulates a hunch I've always believed. In this collection, grief and desire are 'cohorts in crime.' Through the mythic, ritualistic, and the pastoral; by way of transformation and transmogrification; under the aegis of Jorge Luis Borges, Gabriel García Márquez, Federico García Lorca, Brigit Pegeen Kelly, Hammer Horror, Batman, and French New Wave cinema, Cassells has built not simply a collection, but an altar in praise of Longing and its pas de deux with long-legged Time—in the end, that greatest of heartbreakers."

TOMMYE BLOUNT
author of *Fantasia for the Man in Blue*

"Sparks fly, empires fall, and mandolins sing in this transatlantic gospel of seduction as we follow the poet through bamboo labyrinths and secret caves into the arms of the Beloved in an unforgettable lieder cycle of praise. We are all invited to celebrate in this cosmopolitan journey of the 'getaway soul,' wherein Cassells risks and achieves the impossible: a Western romance that ends not in death, but passion, rebirth, and redemption."

VIRGINIA KONCHAN

author of *Bel Canto*

IS THERE ROOM
FOR ANOTHER HORSE
ON YOUR HORSE RANCH?

Is There Room
For Another Horse
on Your Horse Ranch?

POEMS

CYRUS CASSELLS

FOUR WAY BOOKS
TRIBECA

LIBRARY OF CONGRESS CATALOGING-IN-PUBLICATION DATA

This book is manufactured in the United States of America and printed on acid-free paper.

Names: Cassells, Cyrus, author.
Title: Is there room for another horse on your horse ranch? : poems / by
  Cyrus Cassells.
Description: New York, New York : Four Way Books, 2024. | Summary: "Is
  There Room for Another Horse on Your Horse Ranch? Cyrus Cassells Four
  Way Books 2024"-- Provided by publisher.
Identifiers: LCCN 2023031686 (print) | LCCN 2023031687 (ebook) | ISBN
  9781954245808 (trade paperback) | ISBN 9781954245815 (ebook)
Subjects: LCGFT: Poetry.
Classification: LCC PS3553.A7955 I8 2024 (print) | LCC PS3553.A7955
  (ebook) | DDC 811/.54--dc23/eng/20230714
LC record available at https://lccn.loc.gov/2023031686
LC ebook record available at https://lccn.loc.gov/2023031687

Four Way Books is a not-for-profit literary press. We are grateful for the assistance
we receive from individual donors, public arts agencies, and private foundations
including the NEA, NEA Cares, Literary Arts Emergency Fund, and the
New York State Council on the Arts, a state agency.

We are a proud member of the Community of Literary Magazines and Presses.

for "Ben-Him"
ab imo pectore

My eyelids sink toward sleep in the hot
Autumn of your uncoiled hair.
Your body moves in my arms
On the verge of sleep;
And it is as though I held
In my arms the bird filled
Evening sky of summer.

KENNETH REXROTH
"When We With Sappho"

CONTENTS

I. You Be the Dancer

In the small hours, under Taurus,
Let's go back to adoring
The soul of the moon-bathed hill,
Whether we're feeling frisky,
Empty-handed,
Or still beguiled by inchoate dreams—
Let's revisit the cornerstone hour
When, all of twelve, I confessed
My preening babysitter,
In his detestable paisley cap
And sun-faded overalls,
Forced me to be his faux valentine,
And, in a risk-taking gambit,
You grasped my shaky hand,
And led me to this spellbinding hill,
With its exhilarating shouts
Of sage and cinquefoil—

Long ago, amid pert rosemary flowers,
I had my first authentic kiss
(I don't count the bully!),
My first Cuban cigar
(Not the counterfeit bubblegum kind).
As brash, brand-new acolytes,
We had no elucidating word
For the hothouse link between us;
Bud-green Romeo & Romeo, we weren't
Blundering interns:
More like callow troubadours,
Meek or incautious
Navigators of the flesh—

Can you worship a place?
The way the avid Romans once revered
Their tutelary gods?
Look, here's our unmistakable boxwood,
The Blue Star juniper,
The night-silvered belvedere
Revealing the acrobatic river
And the bumpkin town
We were so hell-bent to leave:
I'm sure I could whip up a passable map,
A crude miniature
Of this facile-to-memorize hill,
Our hush-hush stronghold,
Or better still, an apt
Corsair's or scalawag's design,
Reclaimed a century or two from today,
With a conspicuous x-marks-the-spot
Leading its lucky finder
Directly to our talismanic hill—

And yes, this pulse-altering place
Was tantamount to an idyllic schoolhouse:
You praised, like a pimpled Solomon,
My terrific lashes,
My magnetic "tea-brown eyes,"
And taught me to dance on the hilltop—
Mashed Potato, Loco-Motion, Frug, and *Shimmy*—
And thus, mon amour, I found my métier;
You started calling me Dancer,
And the puckish nickname stuck:
I became the nimble boy
All the doting 8th grade girls desired
On the auditorium floor,
But with you, I was a clandestine dancer—

Then in-a-dash years passed:
Some bereft of any word of you,
Some brimming with up-to-the-minute bulletins
Of your escapades, blazing hopes, accomplishments—

Home now, standing on our failsafe hill,
I insist: *Baby, it's worth our while*
Coming back, despite the old
Boredom, secrecy, and blatant bullying—
After relishing the compass star's clarity,
The glittering river's ballet,
You laugh and cajole:
I definitely prefer the grown-up you,
But wonder: can you still manage
A cartwheel? And dare I ask—the Batusi?
To swipe Boy Robin's praise:
You shake a pretty mean cape, Batman!—

Transformed by winnowing Time's wand
Into abiding, grey-bearded revenants,
Burly, truth-or-bust men,
We laugh in disbelief:
Look at us; I can't believe
We're lovers again at sixty—

And on this allaying hill,
Hemmed with showy, Mars-red berries
Littering a reflecting creek,
The hallowing summer night,
The ecstatic hour of our homecoming winds
The way a caduceus winds and heals—

Of course I'll marry you.

MY ONLY BIBLE

is this blood-red joy
Of breathing beside you

And never divining
Your next beguiling voilà:

For instance, the nubile lemon
You culled in Sóller,

Brand-new husband,
Shines, sun-blond and solid,

On the sill,
Pure as a murex shell

Or a nomad's wish—
No wind whistles down

From the timeless sierra,
So after our solstice vows,

You press your apt citrus's
Soothing, gently cooling rind

First to my lips,
Then my slightly sunburned nape—

Finally setting it to rest
On my shirtless torso;

With this honeymoon abracadabra
As nimble cue,

Let me linger and praise
The hermitage and gleaming groves

Above the cobbled village
Where your foxglove-loving mother was born,

The gospel of bougainvillea
At your boyhood gate—the apotheosis,

Bridegroom, balm-giver,
Bell-clear dreamer,

Of your own full blossoming,
And transfixing flair,

Of the soul's endless, luxuriant
Coming and becoming . . .

ACT OF GRATITUDE

from the Catalan of Francesc Parcerisas

Thank you, angel. Thank you,
Demons of the night.

Thank you, winter,
Season in which the heart burns

Arid tree-trunks of desire. Thank you,
Bracing cold light, nocturnal water.

Thank you, stroke-of-midnight bile,
Laurel of the earliest hours, hoopoe of dawn.

For what's odd, unexpected, wild,
For hard-at-work malice and pain, thank you.

For the sum of what we are
And are not,

For all we avoid
And the countless things we crave.

Merci for the lush words
Love and *silver*,

For yourself and myself.
Thank you for full-on yes and deflating no.

For the ability to give thanks
And for rendering them unnecessary.

Oh, gracias for almighty fear,
For shoring bread and oil,

For getaway night time.
Thank you for lovemaking

At day's scintillating hem, for the dollar bill
Plucked from the ground,

For your deft hand on my cheek,
The gush of an ecstatic fountain.

Thank you for your wide-awake eyes and lips,
For crying out my name with joy.

Everlasting thanks, Lord Death,
For your existence,

For making all these things
More vivid inside me—

So very yours,
So beautiful, brimming, and complete.

MAPLES ANTICIPATING THEIR AUTUMN COLORS

Yoshi, at your sudden death,
What stays under my lids, in my body,

After decades: how we biked
The placid length of Kannonji,

Pedaling past ample rice fields
And Shikoku's ramshackle docks,

The ragtag blue stacks
Of an imposing factory in the distance—

Beside an uphill shrine,
Its irrepressible maples anticipating

Their vibrant autumn colors,
We found an unlikely vendor

Hawking Cokes and gimcrack prayer beads,
His piped-in *koto* music

Sinuous among the pines,
A midsummer effort to conjure

The melancholy female ghost
Who lingered and sang on the glinting slope,

Her inescapable voice calling down a god
In the form of a crane,

Its white wings dripping
The cool water of Ursa Major—

THE BAMBOO LABYRINTH

There's nothing you can see that's not a flower;

nothing you can ponder that's not the moon.

BASHŌ

Legions of rice stalks and midsummer reeds
Swayed in accelerating wind. In love,
I followed you all the way to Sado Island.
Fleeing a farrago of Taiko drums,
In favor of the earliest assembling stars,
We laughed and ambled in the twilit
Silver and jade-green field
With our flimsy muslin shirts
Unbuttoned to reveal,
As if to Lothario Jupiter,
The Big Dipper, and the pockmarked moon,
Those old-time eavesdroppers
And unregenerate voyeurs,
The truant glory of our saké-splashed
Collarbones and throats—

An entrancing garland of lights shimmered,
Festooning the flowing Sea of Japan—a little broadcast
Brilliance from Korea (or Manchuria?)—
And almost straightaway, baleful clouds
Came along to block the ebullient stars.
With a shower in locomotion our way,
We hurried to a standstill battalion
Of hallowing trees;
So help me, I'd never encountered
Living bamboo, and by chance,
There was a whole god-sent grove
To revel in—

When the flat-footed, rummaging storm,
The Kabuki-wild rain reached us,
We weren't abject or enraged,
Like bull-headed Lear roughly booted outdoors
By his thorny, repudiating daughters;
We were antic, July-giddy—

Lighting flashes. The swoosh of wind
Rattling the gallant trees, the green and ocher
Auspices of the grove,
Ambushing the soldier-tall spears
Encircling us.
Your pretext was to hold and protect me
From the spieling tempest,
Then you pressed your storm-moist palm
To my novice's chest,
My shield-less heart.
In the tensile year leading up
To that crazy, whistling bamboo maze,
I'd labored carefully to conceal
The sparks I felt so often in your presence;
Like dispensing with an intricate mask
At uproarious Venetian Carnival,
All at once, our mutual longing
Was pond-clear, ineluctable:
No ardent valentine had ever dared
To bless me with a French kiss
Or to probe my wet but febrile nipples
With a purposeful tongue,
And, well, that was an epiphany!

Yes, I admit: I'd never known
The rain-slicked mustache
And black tussock of thick hair,
The telling heat and reassuring heft
Of a man's sinews firsthand—

The wide-awake pilgrim, the not-shipwrecked
Philosopher manqué in me insists:
We outwitting survivors
Return from oblivion or tempest
Out of the ruckus and voltage, alive,
Only to find unmistakable signs,
Indelible memories branding us
Like Lichtenberg figures:
The fabled marks, the improbable flowers
Pitiless lightning leaves
On startled, inconsolable flesh—

Tell me, you, who never attained
Christ's age—my sweet summer despoiler,
Did an errant thunderbolt claim me?
Did I die there in that rain-washed grove?—

All I know is,
My irreplaceable first man,
My amorous prize in the storm,
I can't relinquish our windblown
Bamboo labyrinth,
I can't rest without reclaiming
That bonanza of rain on my flesh—

SPRING COMES TO THE CITY OF LISBON

The tiled city was first
An autumn queen, then a winter one—

City of scattering Sunday vowels
And mourning doves,

City of amethysts and pawnshop gold—

*

Her regal, abruptly revealed flesh,
Her light-holding hills,

Pallid at times
As a lulled baby's bunting

Or a fetching bridal veil—

*

In unsettled and chilly February,
In forever-shifting March,

The ash-white fog of the metropolis
Abrades the stymied harbor ships,

Then slyly erases the famous
Spic-and-span streetcars—

*

City of bold-as-you-please accordions
And irrepressible mutts, wet-nosed Sherlocks

That drift from plate to almost-bare plate
Cluttering low sidewalk tables—

*

City of kite-high hopes,
Of brash-as-rollicking Jove's legerdemain—

*

Libidinous city where I savor
The scent of vetiver in enterprising Manuel's

Murder-to-resist hair—

Now there's a symbol of us,
Manuel grins, pointing to a piebald wall;

I Hate Mondays scrawled in English
Beside *Death to Fascism* in Portuguese!

*

City of *inasmuch* and *moreover,*
Of impossible-to-dismiss mandolins—

*

City that has seldom seen
A vandal-swift snowfall steal

The color from its vaunted streets—

*

City of unhindered fireflies
And ennobling mentors—

*

Never-stern capital
Where Manuel and I spot,

On a clement Ides of March,
Our local panhandler shamelessly

Reveling in the supplanting
Sun on his sullied forehead,

As if to herald the first farewell
To storm-addled winter,

As if to glean, at parade rest,
That passion-braided-with-ease

Which is the exulting river's signature,
The city's prize.

IT'S YOUR FAVORITE FOREIGN MOVIE

—The headlong classic in which July's
Leafed-out lindens & the greengage hill

Spell the end of time & break-spirit yearning:
All the cuckoo-clocks & wristwatches halt,

Even the cosmic mime exploring
The invisible with his expressive hands,

For the adamant, all-systems-go,
Bantering lovers who spy

A furloughed Belgian soldier tumble down
An intoxicating meadow,

Frolicking with his April-named daughter
(O her blossoming laughter

& the riverbed gold of her sunlit hair)
With such wave-crest glee & ecstasy,

The gargantuan future
& the vast, refractory past—*presto chango!*—

Vanish all at once—

HOW MANY LIVES HAVE WE LIVED IN PARIS?

We've lived the life of an unbridled boy
Mastering the higgledy-piggledy metro,

Tapping the fast-moving window,
Loving the a cappella names

Of the heralded stations:
Saint-Paul, Bastille, Gare de Lyon—

*

The life of a downtrodden clochard,
Sly, indigent alley crone

Still wrestling to recover
A long-deterred tune:

Chevalier, dauphin, Parisian charmer,
Don't you know I'm blue without your wink?

*

The life of a pendant, park-facing willow,
Oh sweet, avuncular life—

*

Incarnation of a curling swan—

*

The life of an insouciant schoolgirl
Boulevard-prancing then skipping

In the candle-pale voile of her lark-
Light Corpus Christi dress

*

Life of a heartfelt nun whispering novenas
And bidding God's blessèd day adieu—

*

The taciturn, time-and-again life
Of a ringlet-haired racehorse

On a raucous kids' carousel:
Its red-gold, undignified Sundays—

*

Fat life of a tantalized basilica tomcat
Chasing a fly-by-night sparrow in the pews—

*

The jubilant life of a sweetheart, answering
Yes, oh yes, I will,

Mon amour, *trésor,*
You can toss your hat now into the air—

IS THERE ROOM FOR ANOTHER HORSE
ON YOUR HORSE RANCH?

In schoolboy French, I mentioned
I lived and labored on a horse ranch,

Sequestered in the sun-drenched, verdant
Hill country of Texas.

Later, beside the ample wine table,
Serge-Antoine peered at me,

Through his sensational bangs,
And whispered in alluring, accented English:

*Is there room for another horse
On your horse ranch?*

*

Tell me, when will the Beloved come—
And how?

Picture the selectable doors
In that dreaming-aloud girls' board game

Mystery Date:
Will he be a dream or a dud?

*

Mystery Date, who the hell are you?
A Parisian Papageno?

Mr. Pee Shy?
A metropolitan Dracula who never spies

The Ferris wheel dawn and the pell-mell
Drops of glistening dew?

Don Juan's incorrigible
But surely eye-catching son?

A surfer slash hula dancer who adores
Both ketamine and Shakespeare?

*

If only you could assemble all your lovers,
Achim mused one evening,

With those you desired
But never touched, arrayed

Like ancient Chinese clay guardsmen:
Unearthed, unimpeded,

At-the-ready for your soul's inspection ...

*

When I encountered Dominique in Paris
At the beguiling gypsy circus,

We discovered, so help me,
Both of us had paused

That sultry summer evening,
Like marchers at parade rest,

At precisely the same rakehell page
Of *Tropic of Cancer*—

On day number one of the heat wave,
The lamentable canicule,

On our first outing, Dominique and I ate
Melting crème brûlée, reading aloud,

In sea-colored tank tops,
Raffish passages of Miller's rambunctious classic

In a willow-cloaked niche of a Left Bank park's
Immaculately manicured lawn.

*

That August Dominique cooled his heels
On the ninth floor, dramatically bereft

Of a functioning elevator,
On the Boulevard Saint-Germain-des-Prés,

So to bolster my humdrum trek
To his upraised room,

I'd recite passages of un-shy Sappho
Or soothsaying Lorca's enrapturing

Gypsy ballad that begins:
Green, how I love you, green,

Up, up the unending steps.
Listen, the irksome climb was worthwhile,

If only for the soul-enhancing bells
Of the venerable church of Saint-Sulpice

And our sublime coupling:
Angelsex, I dubbed it, in secret,

After Dominique proclaimed,
In Pernod-fueled English,

On my answering machine:
This is your wanton angel calling . . .

*

I was a virgin with men,
Much greener than Rhett,

And his sex was so much
Thicker than mine:

Vive le différence, he proclaimed,
In zesty, Pepe Le Pew mock-French.

But yours, he said, consoling the novice,
Yours has a beautiful head—

*

That first blustery Christmas in Paris,
I had two Alsatian lovers,

One with peerless gray-green eyes, and the other
With careworn hazel ones,

So my holidays, my *Joyeux Noël* were a windfall
Of scrumptious Alsatian wines, liqueurs, and pastries.

*

An unabashed romantic,
A fanatical cinephile,

Over dessert, canny Jean-Yves revealed
That many of his top-ranked films

Had couples in the titles:
Jules and Jim, Henry and June,

McCabe & Mrs. Miller ...
And we were charmed.

Later, on the divan we relished
The dark coins of his sensitive nipples

At the same time: *his favorite vice,*
He grinned.

Just you, Jean-Yves—
Blowing through our marriage

Like a mistral,
And for a brief season,

We were Jules and Jim and Catherine.

*

After making love for the first time, Paul,
After years of chatter-happy friendship,

I remembered, with inmost wonder,
I was born with your name:

How, on the third day, my parents jettisoned
Their initial choice to honor

An enlisted uncle, a promising sailor
Who perished in the Pacific Theater.

*

The beautiful *signor* waylaid me first
In a museum in Florence, an errant,

Desultory tour guide
For some marveling Catholic students,

Then years later, in a slimmer version
(I didn't recognize him at first!)

While I was strolling along
The ancient Appian Way in Rome—

Last summer I encountered him again
In an imperial room

Of the Pope's Palace at Avignon!
How many times can you run into one man?

*

A little song of homesickness:
Near a Roman metro,

All the livelong summer,
How I prized the bronzed shoulders

Of Nassor, the Egyptian cigarette-seller,
And his ever-inviting smile.

How his eyes flashed
And his handsome face fell a little

When he learned
That I didn't hail from Cairo.

*

Then, in a Moscow apartment,
Marina took first my face then Ilya's

Between her discerning hands
(Even before Ilya and I became lovers)

And motioned to the other guests:
Look, just look at these

Matching cheekbones,
Everyone, pure theater!

Ilya, blushing Ilya,
Who, over the passing years, would shower me

With postcards of dauntless, Stalin-resistant
Boris Pasternak,

The poet's gallantry and probity
Captured at different ages:

This is how you'll look
At forty, at fifty, at sixty!

*

After a bleak, mostly grief-marred March,
I reopened your letter:

Did I tell you how proud of you
I felt at your reading?

And later, in bed together,
With Jean-Yves?

I was, and still am:
I love you . . .

*

If you're prosperous as Midas
Or a busy scion,

If there's room for another stallion
In your capacious stable,

I love you, like wandering Odysseus's
Revenant ship,

Reaches your allaying headlands,
Your longed-for Ithaca,

Again and again.

A TROUBADOUR IN GIRONA

What's said in praise of Romeo is true
Of this young Catalan's absorbing song:

It's new snow discovered
On a raven's back—

All the dusk's redeeming chords,
The cool, lauding coins

Tossed in a disheveled guitar case
Belong to this inspiriting seer—

In the scalloped basilica's
Cloak-like shadow, or in the lustrous

Gardens of the French Woman,
His voice, in old cobblestone Girona,

Has the ingenious sheen
Of just-seen Andorran blossoms,

Something arrow-sure and willing
As an oh-so-purposeful nun,

Or a startling dove, flown
Far from the dovecote—

FULL MOON RISING OVER ISCHIA

I. SECOND HONEYMOON

Beyond our bracing belvedere,
The ink-black bolt of the sea,

Seen through a twilit tournament
Of jousting olive branches—

My work-weary, earth-claimed love,
What a carnival of bougainvillea

Brightens our getaway cottage:
Oh, we've marched here

From the hope-crushing world to this flowery
Castle-keep of purple—

Suddenly christened as knights,
Allies of the grail of joyous purple!

Dearly beloved, a few days later,
We've hardly left the span

Of our fortress-facing terrace;
We've followed so many missives

Of the lustrous sea,
Such a panorama of clashing moods

And windblown colors,
We've had little impetus to explore

The lush remainder of the island,
Though, on a whim, we flagged down

A slow-climbing bus to Barano,
In time to witness racing clouds

Leave ornate shadows,
Lovely patterns on the coruscating sea—

II. MOON-DRENCHED SPAT & GETAWAY

On the starry belvedere,
All night I tossed and turned

On a hammock latched to avuncular island olives:
Restless after a surly cannonade,

A rapid-fire round of accusations:
No more Gethsemanes!

No more pieces of silver!—
But now we sparring lovers are cued

To a honey-tinted moon that blooms,
The inlet's hardy fishermen inform us,

Just once in a hundred years—
Then, in a generous fillip of courtesy,

Four island stevedores are happy to loan us
A you-boys-go-work-it-out white boat—

Meant to hush our rankled lovers' quarrel
With a silvery path toward Vesuvius—

Love, still possible love,
When did trumpet-clear truce

And nighttime caprice
Beat the nosey gossipmongers,

The doomsayers lodged under our lids, to become
The first sure pennants of summer?

HORSEMEN WATCHING TWO ANCIENT CITIES BURN

In the dawn-lit underworld
Of my summer dream, we've taken

The agile horses from the corral;
We've bridled wind-ferried Rommel

And fleet, unfailing Anne of a Thousand Days,
And via some wayfarer's compass

Cached under my closed lids, I sense
We're at a gallop on the master-less,

Glass-green periphery of Rome,
In the ageless countryside near

The long-enduring Christian catacombs
And mast-tall cypresses

Lining the never-say-die Appian Way—
Out of the indomitable blue, I whisper

Roger Wilco, and all at once,
We diligent horsemen hear

A gusty fanfare,
Then an unmistakable rumble

Arriving from the triggered,
Poppy-strewn South—

And soon we spy the transiting,
Scattering breath of irate Vesuvius

Cloaking a pair of entwined lovers,
Trapped forever in Pompeii—

We have no detectable trace
Of the embalmed couple's propelling

Fright or back-and-forth tussles,
Only their spectacular,

Immortalized embrace—
And now Rome—*intricate matron,*

Inveterate cosmos—is visible,
Marred by ascending flames

And immoderate smoke
Fanned every which way,

Yet our intrepid horses remain at peace—
Does this gorgon-red and prophet-

Blue hallucination mean
We're meant to juxtapose

Our still tenacious bond
Beside a sputtering empire's

Spectacular collapse—Look!
The selvage of the looming sky,

Long-dead rider, is diva-indelible
But feral, streaked with lamp-black

Plus lush fringes of carmine—
Dear palm-reader,

Far-seeing dream diviner,
Gone from this flawed earth forty years

(Alas, I only claim you now
In pre-dawn dreams)—tell me,

Where is Nero's trusty fiddle
In this oh-so-combustible world?

FADO FOR XAVIER, THE MOVE-ALONG MAN

When the balmy breeze retreats,
And bound-for-glory clouds,

Crooner, love-maker, it's bitter to feel
The lie of the bullying sun's

Mock-embrace, the dispiriting hush
Of windless moments on the sloping,

Sun-blessed avenues and hills
Of the lyrical-no-longer city—

Listen, I loved a man who captained
A sporty, mint-green convertible

(Oh, his greens were very green!)
With a Valhalla-or-bust magic,

So I slipped in straightaway and wed
My far-ranging fool's quest to his:

Handsome sir,
What are you running from?

Turn your back to the front seat,
Dashing Xavier commanded,

So, without further ado, I stood up,
Raising my sleeveless arms

Under the super-subtle lindens,
As if to nab a glimpse

Of his invisible nemesis, his shadowy
Goliath in the distance—

Imagine, I worshipped a man
Whose aura was akin

To a firm but scalable mountain—
A kind of slapstick earl,

With an inquisitive owl's glance,
But the allure of conquerable worlds

And mast-rich seaports,
Of kestrel-swift wanderlust,

Finally whisked his inimitable soul
Faraway—

I was a lieutenant to a move-along man
Whose enduring homeland was gilded

By a lucent coast
And a much lauded river

Where even a bald-faced lie
Had the splendor of unblemished truth,

But Time and the wind and the river
Took him . . .

DÉTENTE (HERE COMES THE COLD WAR AGAIN)

after Pawel Pawlikowski's *Cold War*

Love, love, we've lost each other again,
And the way back to benighted _____,

To garlic braids, fibs, and stoic folktales,
To drunken arias and rash regimes,

O transiting maestro,
Is a bomb-fissured bridge,

A blasted fountainhead,
A careworn, razor-lipped pledge.

Among Turk's-cap lilies,
Forget-me-nots, and allium blossoms, amour,

You're as subtle as a pterodactyl's swoop,
A rhino's tusk,

Or a cell-wielding,
At-a-gallop Genghis Khan—

Sans all the guile and rollicking cruelty:
Imagine that: a civil Genghis!

Say something!
Escape artist, un-budging soul, don't tell me

This midsummer noon's
Cloud-blessed and never-ending,

Then nimbly execute your spur-
Of-the-moment legerdemain,

Your lick-fast getaway,
Leaving me rudderless, wary,

Bereft of even a telltale
Message in a bottle—

Lovers who've never seen
The ho-hum insides of a jail

Or spied through a Judas-hole,
Inglorious defectors, when we say *yes,*

When an innocuous bouquet,
Like a blameless marital bribe,

Adorns our peace-talk table, replete
With just-baked bread and basement jam,

And a full, frictionless détente
Reigns, suffusing our no-longer-

Feuding household,
Then your flat-out propaganda,

Flagrant morning love-cries,
Your sorrow and your wayward sex

Are all mine—
Even your clove cigarettes

And irresistible hashish
Stashed in the pantry breadbox.

My dove, don't belittle the battlefront,
Don't struggle to dispel

The pillaging soldiers; it's clear,
In the strife-torn, penultimate reel,

Ta-da—it's you!
You're the intransigent enemy,

The menacing catapult,
The mastodon towers

And inveterate sentinels,
Poised and ready to un-kennel

Chaos—the fearsome barracks
And fluttering battle-flags—

Dear headstrong spouse,
I hope our lithe and greedy

Offspring, our stuttering,
Straitlaced-as-Pilgrims

Grandchildren issue a toast
To that unbridled wedding day

When we dipped and swirled,
Galvanized by lightning jazz

And Piaf's "La Vie en Rose,"
Dancers in a sober-seeming village,

Rife with windfall apples and pears,
With rumors of wayfaring bums

And silver-bullet-slain werewolves:
Man and woman blessed

In a humble stone chapel,
Now desolate and in ruins—

Where the cobwebbed, plain-Jane altar
Once gussied with roses

Is wrecked, dull as a boy's
Hapless mitten,

Sullied with straw and snowmelt—
Where the caulked door

Has blown utterly open,
Where the roof's not an actual roof—

Here comes the twister!—
But the brash and streaming sky—

BLOOD RUSHING TO A KNIGHT'S HEAD

As in a tensile joust,
In which stouthearted knights,

Beribboned favorites of the king,
Both dauntless competitors,

Never dare to reveal
The turret-tall stakes,

Time and again, in the eventful years
Following college, I shook

Your firm, almost hallowing hand,
Tallying in my head

Your dynamic triumphs with the requisite
Courteous detachment

(Yes, indifference was the hunter's snare,
The focused angler's reel

Of our later encounters,
Mock indifference and its cousin, nonchalance)

So as to outfox, longstanding crush
And university rival,

You, with your lightly disguised,
Yet thoroughly transparent

Fix on me
(All of your ingenious bids

To secure my applause—detectable
Emblems of an undeclared desire),

Taking note of the inimitable plays,
The sublime films,

The gold and silver accolades,
All you had so diligently attained,

Sometimes with cast-ashore envy,
Sometimes with welling joy—

I see now: under my feigned politesse,
My false reticence,

Beneath almost negligible white lies, denials,
I bore the crest and chilly armor

That hid irrefutable loss,
The fear, in this bustling life, first of squiring

Then losing you—
Everything in my brisk, meticulous

Waking world arranged
(The humdrum opposite

Of my unhampered dreams,
The valiant world under my lids

In which we pledged gallants
And staunch companions strode,

Inseparable as Damon and Pythias)
Permitting me to venture forth,

Sanguine, princely,
A full-blown leader in my field,

But with my secretly allied,
Irrationally loyal heart insolvent—

When I heard the riveting news
Of your cliff-side crash,

Poleaxed as a bested crusader
Or a suddenly gasping chatelaine,

I actually collapsed
In the fabled medieval quarter of Rhodes—

As if someone had savaged the revealing
Strings of an entrancing harp—deposed

On the blank, cool cobblestones
Near the adamant moat

Of Saint John's Gate, toppled
By the sound of your questing voice

In sophomore astronomy class:
What is this colossal force,

This mighty God-spark
That binds the stars?—

So help me, my inmost hero
(Soul-close as a hungry milk brother),

My terrific, quite humbling swoon
Was equal to the noon-struck moment

In a long-ago copse,
When a veering Roosevelt elk

Leapt before me,
As if the astonishing beast could toss,

With its imposing antlers,
The gold chrysanthemum sun,

And I staggered back, dear genius,
I staggered back—

II. Like A Bird of
a More Winged World

CORSAIR

(in collaboration with Brian Turner)

Remember, every lover is a corsair seeking glory,
An x-marks-the-spot, a longing for invisible treasure,

Every lover is an end-point and a start-point
In the history of the world, a spark in the bright flare

Of the possible. Our swashbuckling lovers remind us:
Once we were lazing children,

Housebound and shoreless,
With no concept of the sea

But now there's the ocean's blue pool,
Fleet-winged gulls, windblown caravels,

Even spouting whales,
Crow's nests, and clouds like a white armada—

And so, when we relinquish the body's treasure map, our lovers
Discover us the way the sailcloth in the rigging

Fills with the trade winds, from the last of the night's stars
Through the lavish tangerine of dawn, our ships

Gliding over sheets of light-glazed silver.

THE "LAND HO" KISS

This isn't the Ark, this cruise ship,
Though in life, we're occasionally imperiled,
Occasionally jubilant animals on a journey,

Not unlike Noah's recruited camels & safe-kept toucans—
Our ship-provided horoscopes remind us
We're both hard-to-budge

Earth signs (Taurus & Capricorn)
So how did the serene nighttime sea become
Our escalating desire's sponsor

& Venus's "well, what have we here" white gleam,
A busybody governess or duenna?
Stargazer, co-passenger,

I know it's a matter of supreme kismet
When I linger too long on deck
Just to listen & absorb

Your marvelous vintage guitar
The way my mother Isabel always relished
Nat King Cole & Johnny Mathis;

Confession: when I broadcast her ashes
Over the coastline's blue hullabaloo,
So help me, I crooned "Chances Are"—

Night after night between ports-of-call,
The both of us insistent Sherlocks,
Ready-or-not gossips, we banter

Until inglorious wolf's hour

About our equally hurly-burly pasts:
Our make-believe fisticuffs & top-secret crushes.

I even venture singing Simon & Garfunkel's
"Cecilia" & "The Boxer" with you on a minor dare—
My tenor to your baritone—

Your part Welsh, part Métis skin,
Usually chaplain-pale
From Yuletide Montreal, has bronzed

So thoroughly in the puissant sun,
Your upbeat Quebecois posse insists
You could pass for Cuban—

Under Cassiopeia & the leeward stars,
Your chance-taking lips on mine
Are deadsure—paramount & gorgeous

& your coppery flesh runs warm,
My sun-worshipping Magellan.
Is this glorious, precipitous,

"Land ho" kiss—
This immense starboard ecstasy,
The end of figurative storms?

Troubadour, dice-roller, night raconteur,
Where will you lead me—
Like Noah's unerring dove,

Now that you know I'll follow?

THE BOTANIST (IS THERE GAS IN THE CAR?)

Your five languages are five
Available windows—

Like intricate cathedral glass—
When we kiss on the esplanade,

Or clasp hands
In a city cul-de-sac, nighttime slurs

Don't matter to us,
Or contagious hatred—

In your spacious fourposter, I'm an intent,
Exhilarated pioneer

Or a blameless Columbus
(No mercenary ships or blunderbuss!)

On a quest for the giddy secret
Of your bonhomie,

Your diligent spirit's telltale El Dorado,
City graced not with gold

But a litany of April snowdrops,
Jack-in-the-pulpit, bloodroot,

Scilla, and corydalis . . .
Your prepossessing baritone,

Your silver-threaded auburn beard,
Your windfall cock, and gate-tall body

Captivate me,
The great, Houdini-jubilant freedom

I find in your scrupulous hazel gaze,
My Sunday driver and crackerjack botanist,

As you lead me to a milk-pale,
Indomitable plant,

A spiky alpine mademoiselle
Labeled "Miss Willmott's Ghost,"

And it's true:
I *am* haunted for a spell

FISH CAUGHT IN HIS MESHES

Maël, if a portrait painter or a film director asked,
I'd say you resemble

A long-lashed desperado escaped
From a shoot-em-up spaghetti western—

At a pre-dawn hour, you braid
Your prophet-long, anvil-dark hair

To prepare for the bustling sea-work
In MacKelligan,

But home to Williston Island
And heartening Saint John's Shore,

Back at your inherited Five Maple Farm,
Replete with easy-to-cull, edible trillium,

Scrumptious brook trout,
And an impressive potpourri of stately

Elms, willows, and Lombardy poplars,
You let its luxuriant length

Cascade, as you loll
On your live-a-little, sand dollar bedspread

With a Mr. Lazybones flair,
Just for my libidinous sake,

Making a mock-awning of it,
As if to remind me,

In the old Breton dialect,
The true meaning of Maël is "prince"—

Dear teal-eyed, solid-as-a-Doric
Heir to Daddy Neptune's throne,

Don't I brush and struggle to tame
Your always on fleek hair?

Don't I nestle my seeking face
In its maritime farrago

Of nicotine and sea-spray:
Fish caught in its meshes?

My maverick Maël, in my role
As whistling-awhile apostle,

Ecstatic reveler,
Isn't the wild vowel I prize,

When I take you in my mouth,
Equivalent to the prayer

Of the rushing estuary, the amen-
Shout of the exulting sea?

THE DESIRE PATH

So you've taken a break from ex-wives,
Mendicant sons, and adoring,
Sit-on-your lap grandchildren
To follow a desire path
Through the captivating woods
With a newfound male lover—

Sensuous explorer,
It's the first rousing day
Along the glorious springtime riverbank
When you can jettison your cumbersome,
Almost damask-heavy coat
And even the grimmest city lots
And hawkish alleyways seem no longer
Cold and confederate—

Now, rambling on a desire path,
With our Tweedledee & Tweedledum
Clarinet cases, we lament
The worrying, haywire weather:
How the milquetoast winters are mostly
Hesitant, snowless, un-obliging,
And the freakish summers are inglorious
Summers of fire,
Seasons of unprecedented smoke—

Speaking of truant fires
(Ones both within and without),
My brave love, I want to say:
No, your routed prostate cancer hasn't
Diminished your outsized ardor,
Your avarice for life—

Exhibit A: the houseboat you've acquired
You've christened *Whynot*—

Hard or soft, true virility is innocent,
The architect of March-lapsing-into-April love,
The artful magus of mid-morning
Climaxes and ad hoc,
Cherry-on-the-top haikus:

My own tsunami
Your mouth draws me out to sea
Before the great wave—

So what if we're grandfathers?
It's still spring: the preponderance
Of pear and cherry blossoms
Beside the desire path we've trailed
Is still show-stopping:

Dear seaworthy captain of the *Whynot,*
When we dare to fashion
A makeshift bed
To celebrate, a few weeks in advance,
Our mutual Taurus birthdays,
April fools, mischief-makers,
Lears-in-love,
How fallible and beautiful
Are bodies-defying-time-for-an-hour
Have become.

MAN EXITING A MIGHTY FORTRESS

Early in high school, the taunters realized
It wasn't a rib-crafted Eve

Or a world-altering apple
You were after.

In your panic-ridden,
Jerry-rigged routes to school,

It was easier to downplay
Your appearance,

Man whose body resembles
A Muybridge film-motion study,

The contradictory prowess
Of your hill-and-forest trekker's legs

Under nondescript corduroy
Or everyday khakis.

Such an artful, persistent dreamer and evader—
Tell me, have you found your Adam?

*

You sallied into the world seeking love,
And for some, that salient quest seems

Hallowed, offhand;
Not for you—with a bookworm father,

A heart-cloaked mother,
And a busy-as-hell actress for an older sister,

But here you are:
To your stolid colleagues' shock,

You've left behind your stronghold
Of impersonal laptops and ledgers

To assist in a city hospice,
Brand new samaritan unaccustomed

To candor, confession,
And around-the-clock intimacy,

So you who were half-robbed of touch
In childhood,

And veered from it in college,
Must now claim its immeasurable power—

In your up-close-and-personal vigils
With the faltering,

The leave-taking—
The bullied, tender boy's first hope

Turns out to equal
The soul's valedictory request:

To be honored in full
On this rough-and-tumble,

Denigrating earth,
To be valued and held—

And now I wouldn't exchange
Your expansive heart, your soothing

Hospice worker's touch—
Not for a sultan's jade,

Or a mantle of costly Tyrian purple,
Not for a janissary's stolen topaz—

VERSE IN WHICH THE POET'S NEW LOVER CARVES HIM INTO A SICILIAN PUPPET

I. VERSE IN WHICH THE POET'S NEW LOVER CARVES HIM INTO A SICILIAN PUPPET

In Sicily, you paint my Moor's armor
The illustrious gold of a royal gingko
In garish fall, my foraging, wide-awake eyes
The white of glittering feldspar,
Or far-off Andromeda,
My just-fashioned irises the entreating green
Of Van Gogh's "The Poet's Garden."

But my eyes are brown as pennies, I protest
To my newly acquired lover, Marco Angelo,
Ace woodcarver and able puppeteer
Who looks impressively tan and fit
(It's sweltering mid-July)
In his Starsky and Hutch T-shirt,
While he graces my evolving look-alike
With the bull's-eye gaze belonging
To a go-for-glory trapeze artist
Or a galloping circus showman:

Caro poeta, *I'm sure pea-green works better*
For a daring Moor
Or a defiant Saracen.

Marco, I thought you were transforming me,
Like a modern day Geppetto,
Into a hero, a truth-loving, crusading knight,
Your very own high yellow Orlando!

Well, amico, *as you can tell,*
From the latest phase of the pupo,
I have changed my mind.
By the way, the teasing puppet master whispers,
Gently tapping my island-brown forehead:
Are those brows really yours
Or just a Japanese painter's brushstrokes?

II. MARCO ANGELO'S PUPPET MUSEUM TOUR (COME UPSTAIRS)

The incendiary moment our eyes locked,
Marco Angelo was lifting his peony-pink
And Naples-yellow awning,
And after a lush, prolonged stare, Don Intensity,
With his Jesus-long hair, deliberately
Lowered the awning again,
So I was impelled to amble past
His suddenly reopened store
And inviting woodcarver's workshop
Once, twice, before summoning
My All-American stars-and-stripes resolve
To venture inside, where,
As a dumbshow tourist in Ortigia,
The bewitching island offshoot of Syracuse,
I pretended to browse,
Musing just how long I could sustain
My finicky shopper's ruse,
My mostly lust-fueled performance,
Before fleeing, in a clumsy flash,
With a heartfelt *buona sera*—

Finally, in an affable, committed voice,
Marco Angelo proclaimed:
My two brothers and I, we have
A whole collection of rare
And even precious puppets,
Little stages, woodcarving tools, and old posters,
Yes, a museum—
Please follow me upstairs;
Let me show you—

In a cat-quiet corner
Of the remarkable puppet collection, I confess,
I came for the first time
From the pressure of his formidable,
Sinewy arms, from the shock
Of his trimmed, cologne-scented beard
And care-taking tongue:
At one crest in our lovemaking,
Before the countless widened eyes
Of ready-to-be-seen-and-see antique puppets,
He laughed and wrapped
His waterfall of waist-length hair
Like a dark flag around my throat—

*

It became a summer ritual: I'd arrive,
Just as Marco Angelo was closing:
In our daft, eleventh hour re-enactment
Of his salacious museum tour,
Like an appraising collector,
I'd run my assessing hands

Over a few glittering Sicilian knights
And fearsome, "swart-skinned" Saracens—

Once my avid puppeteer
Literally hauled me upstairs, let me
Unbutton his linen shirt and unbraid
His gleaming black hair,
Then nimbly blindfolded me—with a blue,
Hand-sewn scarf from Cefalù—
To let me savor more fully
Our unleashed bodies' veneer
Of sweat and midsummer musk—

III. MY LOOK-ALIKE SARACEN UNDER THE STARS

After a steady month of meticulous carving, assembling,
Sewing on a black and gold-trimmed velvet cape,
And crowning my hard-knock look-alike
With a shiny, sickle-moon helmet,
Marco declares my bearded twin warrior
Is prime to hit the illustrious puppet stage,
Magically erected in a lovely
But mostly roofless building:
In your honor, we'll let you be
The parlatore—*the voice*
Of the wily Saracen leader
Just for a few performances.
It's good you're an actor as well,
Because, amore, *you better sound mean!*

So into the chivalrous world of Charlemagne,
I plunge—the bustling planet of the Sicilian *pupi*,
Brimming with 9th century Parisians,
Invading Tartars, and Saracens
With beloved stock characters:
The loyal, always do-right paladin Orlando,
The dazzling, clash-inducing beauty Angelica,
The ever-scheming witch Morgana …

.

Look! Here I am relentless, dastardly,
Never giving in to the Christians;
Here I am dramatic, wheedling,
A horse's ass

As I sally into battle under the dog day stars,
I laugh and say, *Marco,*
When things get seriously mean:
Just remember, puppet master, deep down,
Like any steadfast poet worth his salt,
I'm a troubadour, yes indeed,
A verse-spouting lover, head to toe,
Never a harsh foe or a prickly fighter!

THEATER OF SWANS AND MYSTERIES

Playwright, what is it that draws us close—
When the world seems at loggerheads?

In a willow-laden detour to Créteil,
A blithe Thursday pause from Parisian stress,

You lure the inspiriting swans to your side
With fillips of fresh bread,

But the Garbo-shy heron refuses
To stir or alight center stage.

It is not unlike the past, the myriad
Plots and characters cached within us—

*

Île des Ravageurs, Île Sainte-Catherine, Île Brise-Pain,
The names of the Lilliputian islands

(Linked by appealing footbridges)
A genial bracelet or a bagatelle's

Initial notes. Along the tranquil Marne,
We launch into your brand-new play

With a duo of intent anglers
As desultory bystanders,

And a stealthy, beaver-like creature
The French call a *copyu*

As a hirsute witness.
You relish the role of a callous,

Up-and-coming businessman,
And straightaway, I shape-shift

Into an "eyesore," a homeless,
Tatterdemalion crone

Loitering in a London Tube station,
Antsy to present a scathing mirror

To the posh Bond Street princeling's
Blistering selfishness

*

This riverine role-playing implies
Our easy theatrical rapport

Is surely bolder, more fathomless,
Than our Puck-giddy or pensive,

Slowpoke or brisk daylight masks—
As fallible dreamers, co-stars,

We're not immune
To ad libs and nighttime shadows:

In shattering dreams, alarums,
You're the little Shoah girl

Whose hiding-place cough and sniffle
Ensnares her whole hounded family;

You're the doomed, headstrong queen's
Miscarried son, the longed-for dauphin

Whose death-in-the-womb unravels
The irascible monarch's ambitions—

*

What does the here-and-now Marne whisper—
With its Maytime retinue

Of gumshoe-inquisitive swans,
Its foraging tenant heron?

On-the-rise dramatist, lush-haired
Phoenix among pendant willows

And resilient water lilies,
Deep green prosceniums,

You possess the art, the wherewithal,
The inner treasure house to fashion

New worlds, to annul
Disastrous history—

Be with me in this life.
Be brave against the ruinous.

Be born.

CONVERSATION IN THE RUINED TEMPLE OF HERA

How can I tell this barrel-chested jogger,
This charming intruder,
That each evening, at dusk's hem,
I'm drawn (as if by silent command)
To Hera's dilapidated temple—
So help me, in hot-to-the-touch July,
Whatever my island plans,
Despite my hopscotch, rather stop-start tourism,
I always wind up here,
In the shady villa of *Mon Repos,*
Beyond the shuttered pre-Victorian mansion,
Always at the selfsame hour,
Musing among the toppled, ancient stones

Kalispera: Good evening!
May I join you in your meditation?

Being more or less a fan
Of charismatic Mediterranean men,
In no time flat, I surrender
To this semi-formal jogger's
Straight-off-the-bat request:
Yes, of course, be my guest.
Feel free ...

For most of us, the meddling gods,
The lulling nymphs, and sagacious centaurs
Seem long gone—so I'm startled,
When I suddenly reveal to him,
In this tumbledown archeological site:
Sometimes when I close my lids,
I can almost spot the imposing dragon

Rumored to be the Greek goddess's
Unfailing guardian.

Oh yes, I've read about the beast
At Hera's beck and call:
I believe his unsettling, not-so-friendly name
Was Python.

Suddenly, I tease this well-built stranger,
(Who unveils his own name as Yorgos,
Whose English is clear, carefully parsed,
And quite passable):
Perhaps you're the dragon,
Changed to a handsome human form?

That's just the sort of thing a poet would ask!

Believe it or not, Yorgos, I'm actually a poet—

Perfect! Bingo, as you say!
I've spotted you before
And desired to meet you—
I like to jog here on summer evenings,
When the island cools down,
So I pushed past the shyness
That so often plagues me
About my inferior spoken English
(Though, I'm proud to declare, dear American—
You're American, yes?—
My reading ability is good).
I'm not a cosmopolitan,
A modern EU sort of Greek;
I've only known this island

And nearby Paxi, and Cephallonia;
Believe it or not, I've never even seen
Athens's busy chaos;
I'm always reluctant to leave Corfu—

Soon, as if on cue, we both
Slip into an expanding silence,
A yogi's calm, chockablock,
To my surprise,
With showering sparks and vast colors—
Until I hear a soothing Yorgos announce:

And now that we've paid
Homage to our still viable goddess,
Let me lead you
From these sacred columns,
To a cleared path
Through purple cyclamen
Down to the hidden beach:
A delightful and special one, known
Only to longtime islanders—

A little spellbound, intrigued
By our out-of-left-field meditation,
Our odd and lovely talk,
But tranquil, utterly tranquil,
I descend with this mesmerizing jogger
To the glittering beach,
But don't feel in the least bit startled
When he nimbly dispenses
With his batik tank top, pulling me
To his remarkable chest
With its appealing, runaway fur . . .

*

When hardy, easy-to-adore Yorgos and I
Climb back to the stones, I confess:
When you were making your moves,
Dear Corfiat, I swear I could sense
The busybody dragon's wings
Hovering above the beach—
How is that possible?

Don't get me wrong:
So help me, I'm no voyeur,
But once upon a time, I heard
The subtle music of your sighs
On the beach at Mirtiotissa—
In a state of wonder,
I stumbled onto the cave
Where two powerhouse men (a swimmer
From Thessaloniki, I believe,
And his bearded lover,
A Cypriot painter)
Were indeed adoring—
In fine, muscled fashion—
The showcase of your sun-golden
Limbs and torso,
Filling you in unison
Just as the foraging tide
Ambushed the cave and gripped
Your supple wrists and ankles …
And from my secret post,
My dragon's perch,
I vowed to have you for myself,
So, in a match-burst, I transformed

Into a masterly lover,
A perfectly alluring mortal—

Dear Dallying Jogger,
Or, to absolutely blast the bull's-eye,
Dear Temple Dragon:
You tricked me!

My sweet, dreamy bard, wouldn't you say
That's just the sort of thing
Irreverent dragons do:
A timeless recipe of lusty fire
Mixed with a pinch of mischief—
Besides, Yorgon insists,
Hera heard your summer prayer,
Your subterranean request
For the nuzzle and thrust
Of a more attentive lover;
Here in this ruined temple on Corfu,
You've been faithful
To the timeless goddess
In the steadiness of your evening visits—
A form of reverence and praise,
So the cloud-borne sponsor
Of sweethearts, brides, and lissome lovers,
Zeus's long-suffering wife
Summoned me—but don't fret,
My delectable poet:
With one dragon's purposeful breath,
I can banish, abracadabra, the joyous
Memory of our beach-time
And fireworks meditation—

When I open my eyes,
The ancient, reliable sun's setting,
The immense park's ready to close:
I'm sitting, blissfully cross-legged,
In the disheveled temple,
Alone among the slipshod columns,
The gorgeous, wrecked pediments:

Yorgos, what? What did you say?

When I spotted eye-catching Stavros,
A man on a joyous carousel:
He was comically saddled
On a cartoon racehorse
With his loudly clapping five-year-old son,
Bobbing up and down
To the loopy music of a calliope
(How do you say *giddyup* in Greek?);
I was entranced, of course,
By his clear-to-all tenderness
And unabashed laughter,
And his puissant, lucid-blue gaze,
Like a salvo—
Tell me, are you a tourist? Yes?
Then you must come to my restaurant
On a hill beside the New Fortress;
Don't forget. Here's my card—

If the evening tables weren't too busy
In his terrific seafood tavern,
Caring Stavros would pause to chat
With "Captain America"
(As he quickly christened me)
Sometimes until closing—
There was a carefree aura
About our late-night talks
And occasional strolls
Through Corfu Town's vital labyrinth:
Balmy, centering, and arousing
In almost the same breath—
That's how I discovered appealing Stavros hailed
From Thessaloniki, not the island—
When he gallantly elected to help me

Improve my less-than-stellar swimming:
Captain America,
It's my specialty, he proclaimed—

As a desert-raised military brat,
I'd learned much too late
To fully tackle the agile butterfly
And essential breaststroke—
So solicitous Stavros,
Once Olympics-headed in his teens,
Offered to instruct me—
A felicitous gesture because
"Stavros is the best swimmer on Corfu,"
Insists his bearded painter friend,
Whom everybody calls Big Iraklis—

Stavros was infinitely courteous, easygoing,
Calmly working with me in a hotel pool,
Until he suggested swimming lessons
At a few western beaches:
Yialiskari, Halikounas, Vatos,
And after a month of exploring
Those genial out-of-town settings,
He finally said: *It's time to hit*
The nude beach, Mirtiotissa;
I hope that's not a problem—

At Mirtiotissa, the shoreline stones
Were just lackluster stones,
Till, in a sorcerer's flash, the tide claimed
Their black and pell-mell pewter—
The high, rugged cliffs,
The multicolored water shimmered,

While the bellicose morning fumed,
Almost sauna-hot,
So the only recourse was to jettison
Our cumbersome shorts
And flower-patterned trunks and welcome
Mirtiotissa's almost lukewarm waves,
Rife with darting, migratory fish—

We strolled past what Stavros tagged
"The textile guests,"
The old sarong-sporting
Hippie survivors from the 80s
When the tantalizing beach
Was much wider—and,
According to local gossip, wilder.
It felt truly liberating
To practice our usual strokes,
Unhampered by any trunks.
While his sidekick Big Iraklis
Dozed and tanned on the shore,
Delightful Stavros, minus his clothing,
Was consistently quiet,
Tranquil, and undaunted, confiding:
I feel happy as a clam,
As you English speakers say—

We rested a little after my lesson,
Then Stavros said: *Come, let me show you*
A cave I've found; it's really quite something.
We can leave Mr. Big-Ass Iraklis behind
To sleep and snore.

There were just enough holes
In the outlying cave's rough ceiling
To approximate natural skylights,
So the hovering sun cast a spotlight
To emphasize Stavros's face and cheekbones
As he whispered,
Since you met me with my son,
I'm sure you imagined
I had no desire for you
Or other men, but I do;
I brought you here because ...

There was no resisting courteous Stavros then,
His blue-green, un-ignorable gaze,
His strong, stubble-dotted jaw,
His half-moon scar complicating
His film-star-ideal cleft chin,
His drying torso, still glistening from the sea,
His hardy, suddenly encircling arms,
His white-as-a-hospital-ward teeth,
His insistent lips at my ear's curve,
His cologne-flecked nape and Adam's apple,
His questing, failsafe tongue,
His commanding kisses,
His formidable shoulders and biceps (his biceps!),
His diamond-shaped birthmark almost covering
His left armpit (the sweat and seaside musk my nostrils find there)
His broad chest, meant for worshipping,
His aureoles like bronze zeroes, excavated coins,
His sea-wet nipples like small swart summits,
His salt-tasting index finger between my mock-biting teeth,
His cable-taut thighs, marvelous pillars,
His able cock, arriving like an astute animal—

I heard a sibilant gull's cry and susurrus,
And sensed someone else
Looming in the cave:
Beautiful, Big Iraklis whispered,
Oh, baby, be good to Stavros.
Captain America, do you mind if I watch
And touch you, too?
Iraklis, the gate-tall tagalong, whom I figured
Was mostly indifferent to me!
Admission: his outsized penis
Felt almost amiable at first,
At rest on my sienna-skinned shoulder,
Then thick and thicker
In my grasping hand—

After laving away
Pale pennants from the little battlefield
Of my glistening belly, souvenirs
Of our unhampered horseplay,
At dusk, suddenly dwarfed
By the evening sky,
We danced at the sea-lip
With some newfound friends
To Stavros's many catchy tapes
(*What is this,* I laughed,
Greek Soul Train?), and once,
Between irresistible songs,
And a wild, free-form summer *sirtaki*
(*I'm the king of the castle;*
You're the dirty rascal!),
He whispered:
If you're wondering, I didn't plan on
The three of us in the cave,

But Big Iraklis is always restless,
Curious. And of course,
He was a little jealous!
Now to my real question: it's only
The middle of summer, so you'll still need
More swimming lessons, right?
And our busy painter's suddenly ready
To paint your portrait—
I wonder why!
Knowing him, he'll probably splash
More paint on your American flesh
Than on his waiting canvas!—
So, dear Captain, you must come see us!

More than half-intoxicated,
Weed-struck, an ecstatic Stavros
Rushes in my direction,
Waving the white spine
Of some poor, luckless fish
Like an irreverent movie prop,
Hollering, chanting, almost singing:
Mirtiotissa, Mirtiotissa!
I'm crazy for Mirtiotissa!
With a ribald jester's, a truant's
Face-splitting grin,
Elm-strong Iraklis blurts:
Captain America, for sure,
I'm pretty large down there—
You know, that's how I got
My nickname—so I have to say
I'm impressed!
Have no doubt, as Stavros told you,
I'm planning to do your portrait,

So let's have another round
Of ouzo, or maybe your prefer retsina.
Let's drink a toast to Stavros's 'special cave,'
A toast to Mirtiotissa!

THE WRESTLERS (CARAMELO AND GUAPO GRINGO)

Though I was rash, run-of-the-mill—
A tagalong athlete at best,
How is it, after all these years,
We're still punning and wrestling?
We never banter about this,
The bald-as-a-sumo fact you insisted I drop
"Fancy-pants" French and straightaway "enlist"—
That's exactly the verb you used!—
In "handier" First-Year Spanish,
And then recruited me
For the mostly belittled wrestling team;
I'm sure, for your part, even then,
Disciplined mat-work was akin
To outright philosophy, a pulsing physical form
Of fathomless meditation—

I confess it tickles me you've settled
In "Guadalajara, Guadalajara,"
The vaunted birthplace of our tiny,
At times fortissimo Spanish teacher,
The far-sighted woman who instilled in us
An endless love for totemic García Lorca,
The magus García Marquez,
And blind, encyclopedic Borges—
On Señora Leticia's engaging
High school senior Spanish Club trek
To gargantuan Mexico City,
I fell in love with Montezuma's
Godzilla-and-Mothara-sized metropolis,
But lamented my gadabout paseos,
Without fail, blackened my saved-for deck shoes—

In "onerous" high school,
As we once derided it,
As disapproving sophomores,
You felt half-cursed by your German
And Scandinavian good looks,
And instead of duly squiring
The fig-ripe Valkyries,
The cookie-cutter sweethearts
Your Cologne-born mother
Had carefully, almost gingerly,
Allotted for you,
In wayward fashion,
You praised our high desert town's
Wary, wiseacre Latina girls,
With lush rose-trellis names:
Keris, Jacinta, Maria Isabel, Socorro ...

I replay those early years
Of sheer horseplay and camaraderie,
As we trek to irresistible Tulum,
And later, climb to the panoramic top
Of the rugged pyramid in Cobá
(Yes, with its buffeted cloud flotillas,
Its fabled blue-and-white canopy,
Mexico possesses my favorite sky),
Stopping for a journeyman bullfight
In a humble jungle village,
Where your flagpole-height,
Wheat-colored ponytail,
And tallow-pale forearms
Make you a lightning-fast Nordic celeb,
A Mayan curiosity—

Back in college, we used to exclaim:
I see a hammock with my name on it!
Nowadays, in spiffed-up Playa del Carmen,
There's little sleeping outdoors:
After a flirty jack-of-all-trades
Valiantly fixes your truck's flat tire,
Marcelino gleefully coaxes, and yes, slyly ushers
"Caramelo and Guapo Gringo"
(As if we'd been hailed
As first-class *Lucha Libre* wrestlers!)
To a newly inaugurated, no-frills hotel,
Where an impervious tarantula blooms
Above the lintel of our shore-blessed room,
Like a blossoming black star
In some abysmal Hammer Horror—

In this bright, empty-bellied hotel,
I recall, before our lively tenure
As on-fire teen wrestlers,
The summer-to-summer stretch
That we incorrigible thespians
(Acned, raring to go, and graced
With ever-ready erections)
Started impersonating blood-sampling
"Champs and Vampires"—
Count Dracula versus Barnabas Collins!—
And our delightful horror show duel
Suddenly veered (as if some leering demigod
Or lust-inducing satyr
Had waved a magic wand)
Into our first heedless kisses,
Our first blissed-out thrusts
And quick-as-a-hare climaxes—

As you recall, your tree house
Was aptly christened "Collinwood West,"
(You were obsessed, naturally,
With that creaky-as-a-crypt-lid soap,
Dark Shadows)
And my own cobbled-together perch
Was dubbed Lord Dracula's Castle—

Today we're the untried inn's
Absolute first and only welcome guests,
So nobody but nobody can detect
Or fault my sudden gasps
As our at-ease siesta,
Started in separate beds, becomes
More than your usual Yucatan siesta—

In our marvelous, semi-nervous,
Yet still vigorous faux-wrestling,
Followed by our surprise,
Hello-again coupling,
Hallelujah, you're a man now,
Possessing a roustabout's chest
And impressive shoulders,
And lo, your strong, insurgent kisses
Are much surer than at fumbling fourteen:

Look, how did you get inside me,
Barnabas Collins? Does this mean
We're Champs and Vampires again?

COYOTE SEDUCES A STATUE

One glimpse—that's all,
    Then in no time flat,

Coyote's beguiled,
    Spit-shine kempt:

Cologne-scented singer,
    Bouquet-bringer, acrobatic

Twister into arabesques:
    What can I change?

What's the surefire ingredient?
    How many howls

Make a billet-doux?
    Good luck,

Sings the swan-white moon,
    Good luck & let me know—

    No desert crones,
No love-is-cowbones

    Cynics can quell
His in-a-hurry heart:

    He wants the polestar
As a wedding preacher,

    A cactus for the breakneck
Matrimony's witness,

Brisk Rabbit
To give the bride away—

　　Have you ever felt
Your plumed-chapeau strategy,

Your happy-ever-aftering hid
　　A duncecap desire?

Tell me now.
　　Have you ever found

A glowing storefront rose
　　At closer range

To be the flimsiest, most gimcrack
　　Counterfeit?

Surely once or twice.
　　Have you ever felt your jukebox nights

Collapsing—nod your head if you have—
　　Into migraine dawns,

Like the black pulse of dominoes
　　Dropping to earth?—

On a hot hill's pedestal,
　　On a sky-high hill.

What the snatch-gossip birds,
　　The yolk-bright sun reveals:

The stock-still, not-murmuring lips,
    The stiff, ungenial arms:

Coyote has seduced a statue!

I MET A GLADIATOR (BEN-HIM)

Once upon a time, you worked in a racy bar
Called The Centurion
That required you to dress
In full gladiator regalia,
And on our first nighttime outing,
To my surprise (and thrill!),
You kept the extravagant Roman costume on,
Elegant, comme il faut sandals and all,
Even in the breakneck taxi
And raging disco—

My savvy best friend insisted we meet,
Arranging a blind date—
Something I usually avoid—
And just outside the Brazilian eatery you chose,
Some friends of yours (recognizable movie stars!)
Saluted you and asked:
Why so many clothes, Mr. Model?
Over delicious feijoada, you filled me in about
The Spartacus-themed bar
Where you worked
And your reputation as an ace
At posing for romance novel covers
(To help bankroll law school),
And of course, the fact you were notorious
For roller-skating around Chelsea shirtless—

At a glamorous Tribeca disco you proved to be
A fabulous dancer,
And for the first time in my life,
I felt intimidated; I dialed
Our wise and lovable friend, laughing:
Why didn't you warn me about "Ben-Him"!

I looked into your maverick blue eyes
On the dance floor and thought:
I know your spirit!—

Flash-forward twenty years:
We meet again, and this time
Our matured and tested hearts,
Our timeless and laughter-rich friendship
Seem totally attuned!
Retired sexual saint, former disco superstar
With a once-pleasing posse
Of come-hither actors and pretty boys,
In the 21st century, I like that you're proud
Of your gradually-acquired belly
And almost priestly pate;
Nowadays, I'm an all-out fan
Of your nonstop altruism,
Your multilingual mind
And on-tap fellow feeling
As well as your former champion body;
Legal master-builder who let go
Your *ludus,* your long-ago gladiator school,
And flashy Chelsea Colosseum,
It's clear as a campanile
Or a cornet's register, you've chosen
Your boundless humanity,
Your mountainous and caring spirit,
In favor of your hard-earned biceps,
And oh, that's exhilarating news, Ben-Him,
That's progress—

What in the world—in one earthly sojourn,
Can a forthright man be both
A Hercules and a Mother Teresa?
I'm planning to stay tuned!

The leafless days were warden-stern
Or dollhouse-fragile

During the winter Beautiful Del
Of the summer sandals and I slept

Between the banter of busy owls,
As the indomitable creek below

Our frost-flecked terrace
Whistled, swelled, and dwindled,

According to irascible gusts
Or cannon-grey fiats of rain—

Our invisible woodland debaters
Would begin their counterpoint at dusk,

A feathery Siskel and Ebert;
Who would answer *What,*

And their loquacious tête-à-tête would prevail
To a wild-eyed hour, and beyond—

The last time clear-sighted Brigit
Trekked into town,

She alerted us to a frisking owlet, a fledgling
Lodged in an eave's nest,

A neighborhood arrival we'd overlooked,
Which made discerning Delarue wonder

Whether our duo of effusive owls
Was indeed a creek-drawn, sweet-talking

Romeo and Juliet, forest lovers,
Not gossips or refractory foes—

Brigit was ruby-keen—always vividly attuned
To myriad pastoral and classical worlds.

Over a bay shrimp dinner, she described
Her taskmaster father's instilling habit

Of reading to her, without fail,
The titans —Dickens, Melville, Dostoyevsky—

Pages impossible for a schoolgirl's grasp,
But many birthdays later,

The masters' unmistakable tales and voices
Bloomed, in all their thunderous relevance—

Of course, Brigit's clarion-clear brilliance
Was more, so much more

Than merely updated Pygmalion,
A parrot's or a daughter's

Dutiful mimicry: her genius, a eureka beyond
Sheer indoctrination—

Now that handsome Delarue
And savvy, indelible Brigit

Are both dead, and I dare to open
My cached-away book

Of creek-house joys,
Brimming with wide-awake levity

And a kind of belly wisdom;
I begin to suspect,

Placing its vivacious chapters beside
My locked album of lingering grief,

That the chatter-happy owls'
Nighttime sagas are still stored

In the parkland as buoyant,
Branch-launched gifts;

I begin to dream that I can decipher
The blissful creek-side forum,

The revealing and voluble
Back-and-forth of great horned owls—

All my soul mate's IOUs were sensual,
And his galvanizing cock fit

My eager grip
Like a scepter might.

Don't tell me a man's fabled G-spot
Is merely a fancy ruse, elusive folklore,

A Loch Ness monster!
Confession: when I came clean

For the fourth stupefying time
From Del's on-tap prowess,

His ne plus ultra kisses,
It was as elating

As my twenty-first birthday hug
From the heroic Mister Harvey Milk.

And in our post-coital splendor,
Out of the super-subtle blue,

Tousled bedheads, we began to whistle
For no particular reason—

As if to forestall the blizzard's
Wind-hurled volleys—

The "Colonel Bogey March"
From *The Bridge on the River Kwai*,

As first the dead-of-winter metropolis,
Then the whole vaunted, visible world,

Lord, have mercy on our amassing wonder,
Turned egret-white . . .

LIKE A BIRD OF A MORE WINGED WORLD

Animula, vagula, blandula . . .

(Little soul, charismatic wanderer . . .)

HADRIAN'S DEATHBED POEM

Fly from this cage, like a bird of a more winged world.

RUMI

Retreating turncoat, little ally, tell me,
What will you recall

Of the cypress-blessed earth's gravitas,
Of the jilted body's camaraderie?

Insouciant guest, more than the tangled,
Unsparing world,

Runaway bride,
With your kept-quiet lust

For God's fireworks,
Perhaps you'll garner,

From a massive inner storehouse,
The match-quick memory of a cardboard

Yet weirdly imperial crown
Perched on a milliner's dummy,

The spell of impeccable white peaches
Hauled from fragrant Languedoc orchards,

The glimpse of a breeze-swept passerine
Heading south for sunnier Malta

In a brash swirl of sea and ilex,
In a quest for pine nuts and black cherries—

Freed from shadow-brokers, flesh, you're flight-ready,
Vehement to learn *(Animula, vagula, blandula...)*

Emperor Hadrian's valedictory lessons,
To assess the bracelet of cities

You cherished vicariously and left
As stainless, inviolate—

To salute gone-too-soon lovers,
Surrendered to swaying

Cemetery grasses
During the decimating years,

Marked by cell counts and hospices.
Even your own slim San Francisco Antinoüs—

Imagine he isn't plague-snatched,
But lesion-less, everlasting—

Soul, with your unlimited
Wingspan, your holy egress,

In concert with the sallying crow's
Go on,

The galvanizing owl's farewell,
Sly "fingersmith,"

Unremitting rascal,
Filching a last communion wafer,

As if it were *Maman's* unforgettable
Holiday macaroon:

Oh, getaway soul,
You've been caught red-handed—

I BELIEVE ICARUS WAS NOT FAILING AS HE FELL

You've just died in my arms,
But suddenly it seems we're eternal

Cali boys, Afro-haired cohorts in crime,
Racing through intricate lattices

Of quince and lemon tree shadows,
Corridors of Queen Anne's lace—

On the skip-church Sunday you dubbed me
"Sir Serious" instead of Cyrus—

Then, swift as a deer's leap, we're devotees
Of goatees and showy Guatemalan shirts,

Intoxicated lovers for a month
On the northwest coast of Spain—

Praising the irrepressible sounds
Of a crusty Galician bagpiper

On La Coruña's gripping finisterre,
Then gossiping and climbing

(Like the giddy Argonauts we were)
The lofty, ancient Roman lighthouse,

All the way—*Keep on truckin'*, we sang—
To the top of the Tower of Hercules—

ACKNOWLEDGMENTS

Cover art: "Night Traveler" by Suzanne Betz

"When We With Sappho" by Kenneth Rexroth, from THE COLLECTED SHORTER POEMS, copyright c 1944, 1963 by Kenneth Rexroth. Reprinted by permission of New Directions Publishing Corp.

Many thanks to the Fine Arts Work Center in Provincetown, the Mabel Dodge Foundation, the Helene Wurlitzer Foundation of New Mexico, and to Texas State University for their support. The title poem is for Carole Maso, with love and admiration. "A Troubadour in Girona" is for Joan Xifra Quintana. "The Winter We Slept between Bantering Owls" is in memory of poet Brigit Pegeen Kelly (1951-2016). "Like a Bird of a More Winged World" is in memory of Domingo. The title "I Believe Icarus Was Not Failing as He Fell" is the penultimate line of Jack Gilbert's poem "Failing and Flying." "Act of Gratitude" is a "free version" of a poem that I translated directly in *Still Life with Children: Selected Poems of Francesc Parcerisas* (2019). "Corsair" is a collaboration with poet Brian Turner, as part of his anthology of collaborative poems, *When You Ask for Something Beautiful*.

This book was a finalist for the National Poetry Series.

These poems first appeared in the following magazines and anthologies, some in earlier versions: *Academy of American Poets Poem-a-Day, Agni, The Common, The Cortland Review, Cutthroat 28, Essential Queer Voices of U. S. Poetry* (Green Linden Press), *The Fight and The Fiddle, Ganymede, The Harvard Review, Matter, Nine Mile, Passengers Journal, Ploughshares, Poetry International, Poetry Northwest, Prairie Schooner, Round Top Poetry Anthology* (2023), *Salmagundi, The Taos Journal of International Poetry and Art*, and *When You Ask for Something Beautiful*.

ABOUT THE AUTHOR

Cyrus Cassells was the 2021 Poet Laureate of Texas. Among his honors: a 2023 Civitella-Ranieri Foundation fellowship; a 2022 Academy of American Poets Laureate fellowship to administer his statewide Juneteenth poetry project; a 2019 Guggenheim fellowship; the National Poetry Series; a Lambda Literary Award; two NEA grants; a Pushcart Prize; and the William Carlos Williams Award. His 2018 volume, *The Gospel according to Wild Indigo,* was a finalist for the NAACP Image Award, the Helen C. Smith Memorial Award, and the Balcones Poetry Prize. *Still Life with Children: Selected Poems of Francesc Parcerisas,* translated from the Catalan, was awarded the Texas Institute of Letters' Soeurette Diehl Fraser Award for Best Translated Book of 2018 and 2019. *To The Cypress Again and Again: Tribute to Salvador Espriu,* combining translations, poetry, and memoir in homage to Catalan Spain's most revered 20th century writer, was published in 2023. Cassells was nominated for the 2019 Pulitzer Prize in Criticism for his film and television reviews in *The Washington Spectator.* He teaches in the MFA program at Texas State University, where he received a 2021 Presidential Award for Scholarly/Creative Activities and was named a 2023 University Distinguished Professor.

PUBLICATION OF THIS BOOK WAS MADE POSSIBLE
BY GRANTS AND DONATIONS. WE ARE ALSO GRATEFUL
TO THOSE INDIVIDUALS WHO PARTICIPATED IN
OUR BUILD A BOOK PROGRAM. THEY ARE:

Anonymous (14), Robert Abrams, Michael Ansara, Kathy Aponick, Jean Ball, Sally Ball, Clayre Benzadon, Adrian Blevins, Laurel Blossom, Adam Bohannon, Betsy Bonner, Patricia Bottomley, Lee Briccetti, Joel Brouwer, Susan Buttenwieser, Anthony Cappo, Paul and Brandy Carlson, Dan Clarke, Mark Conway, Elinor Cramer, Kwame Dawes, Michael Anna de Armas, John Del Peschio, Brian Komei Dempster, Rosalynde Vas Dias, Patrick Donnelly, Lynn Emanuel, Blas Falconer, Jennifer Franklin, John Gallaher, Reginald Gibbons, Rebecca Kaiser Gibson, Dorothy Tapper Goldman, Julia Guez, Naomi Guttman and Jonathan Mead, Forrest Hamer, Luke Hankins, Yona Harvey, KT Herr, Karen Hildebrand, Carlie Hoffman, Glenna Horton, Thomas and Autumn Howard, Catherine Hoyser, Elizabeth Jackson, Linda Susan Jackson, Jessica Jacobs and Nickole Brown, Lee Jenkins, Elizabeth Kanell, Nancy Kassell, Maeve Kinkead, Victoria Korth, Brett Lauer and Gretchen Scott, Howard Levy, Owen Lewis and Susan Ennis, Margaree Little, Sara London and Dean Albarelli, Tariq Luthun, Myra Malkin, Louise Mathias, Victoria McCoy, Lupe Mendez, Michael and Nancy Murphy, Kimberly Nunes, Susan Okie and Walter Weiss, Cathy McArthur Palermo, Veronica Patterson, Jill Pearlman, Marcia and Chris Pelletiere, Sam Perkins, Susan Peters and Morgan Driscoll, Maya Pindyck, Megan Pinto, Kevin Prufer, Martha Rhodes and Jean Brunel, Paula Rhodes, Louise Riemer, Peter and Jill Schireson, Rob Schlegel, Yoana Setzer, Soraya Shalforoosh, Mary Slechta, Diane Souvaine, Barbara Spark, Catherine Stearns, Jacob Strautmann, Yerra Sugarman, Arthur Sze and Carol Moldaw, Marjorie and Lew Tesser, Dorothy Thomas, Rushi Vyas, Martha Webster and Robert Fuentes, Rachel Weintraub and Allston James, Abby Wender and Rohan Weerasinghe, and Monica Youn.